A Fin, a Grin, and a Pin

Written by
Howard Wells

Photographs by
John Paul Endress

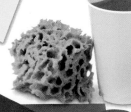

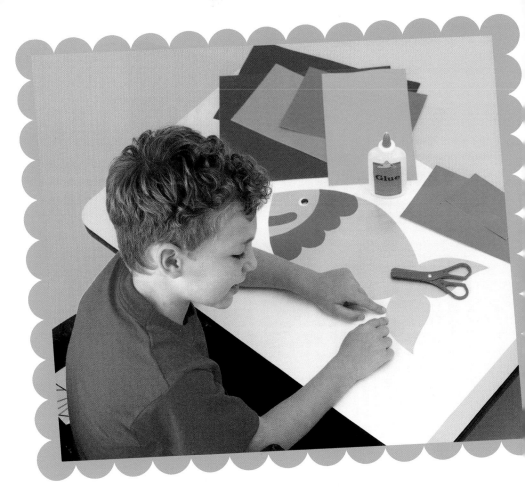

Make a fish

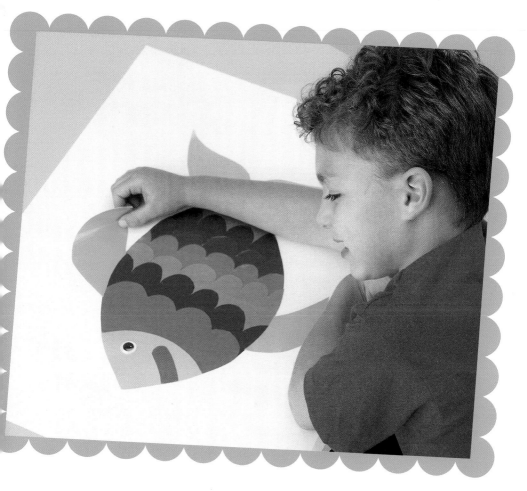

that has a fin.

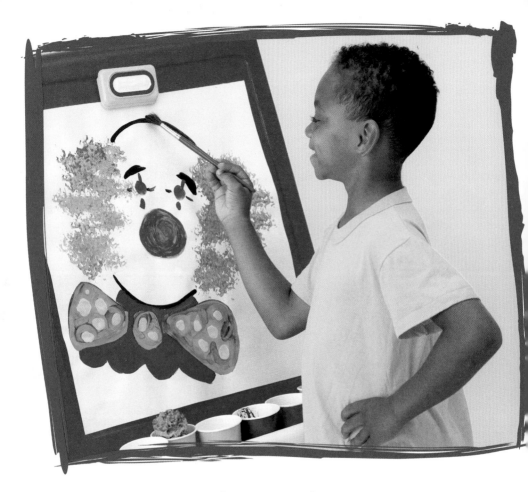

Make a clown

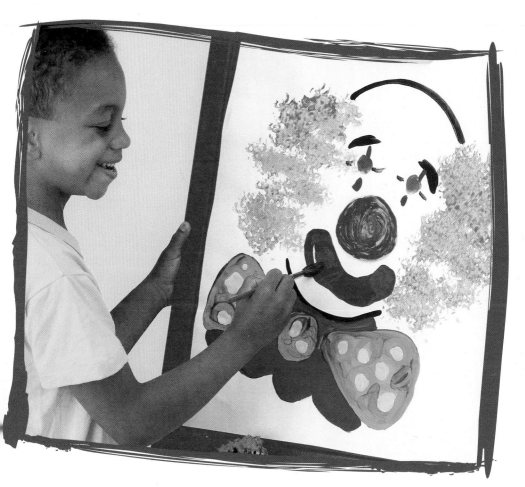

that has a grin.

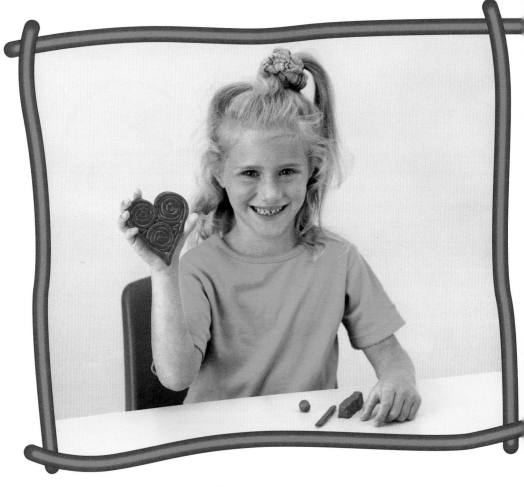

Make a heart

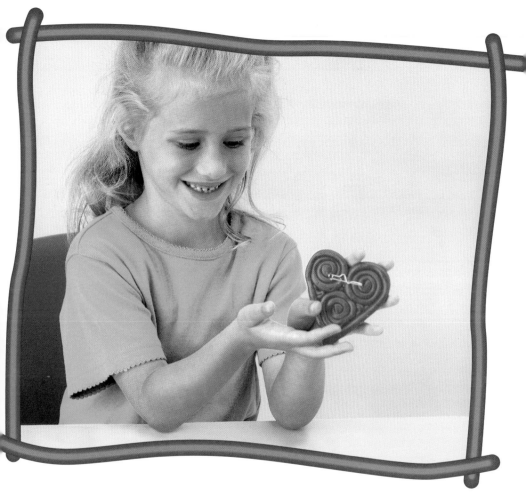

that has a pin.

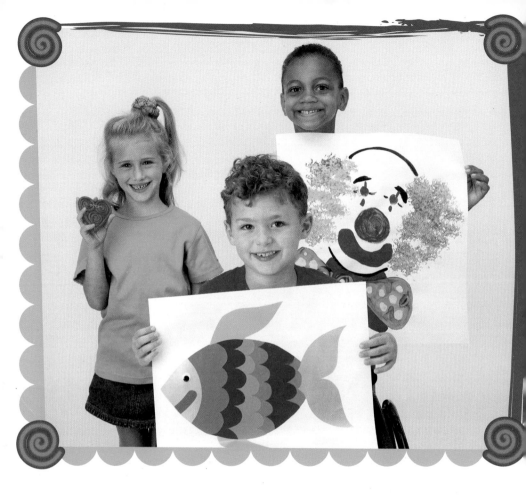

A fin, a grin, and a pin!